*P*RESSURE
*D*RESSING

Mark Scroggins

MADHAT PRESS
ASHEVILLE, NORTH CAROLINA

MadHat Press
MadHat Incorporated
PO Box 8364, Asheville, NC 28814

The Library of Congress has assigned
this edition a Control Number of
2018962191

ISBN 978-1-941196-81-6 (paperback)

Text by Mark Scroggins
Cover design by Marc Vincenz

www.madhat-press.com

First Printing

Also by Mark Scroggins

POETRY:

> Red Arcadia
> Torture Garden: Naked City Pastorelles
> Anarchy

NONFICTION:

> The Mathematical Sublime: Writing About Poetry
> Michael Moorcock: Fiction, Fantasy and the World's
> Pain
> Intricate Thicket: Reading Late Modernist Poetries
> The Poem of a Life: A Biography of Louis Zukofsky
> Louis Zukofsky and the Poetry of Knowledge

EDITED:

> Our Lady of Pain: Poems of Eros and Perversion by
> Algernon Charles Swinburne
> "Additional Prose" in Prepositions+: The Collected
> Critical Essays of Louis Zukofsky
> Upper Limit Music: The Writing of Louis Zukofsky

Table of Contents

This book is, once again, for JL.

Præfatio ad Lectorem

This is a Florentine volume.

You've come to this country to relax and enjoy this beauty and cultural diversity—not to exhaust yourself searching for the best deals and most evocative experiences.

McDonald's.

It is difficult to characterize in brief compass a span of time as long as that in which Queen Victoria reigned over England and her realms beyond the seas.

Ruskin was born in the same year as Queen Victoria, who outlived him by twelve months and two days.

Conceptions of the nature and purpose of art closely parallel man's conceptions of himself and of his destiny.

No doubt by now you've heard the news of Monk's death.

Oscar Wilde: we have only to hear the great name to anticipate that what will be quoted will surprise and delight us.

A man's life is his time: his time a figure in the great historical procession.

When the Wind is fair and the Planks of the Vessel sound, we may safely trust every thing to the management of professional Mariners: in a Tempest and on board a crazy Bark, all must contribute their Quota of Exertion.

I first thought of writing this book when I realized hardly any of the students of literature I encountered these days practiced what I myself had been trained to regard as literary criticism.

The theory of painting, architecture and sculpture which established John Ruskin's influence in Victorian times scarcely outlived his century.

An Academy in which the Polite Arts may regularly be cultivated, is at last opened among us by Royal Munificence.

Data float down; the own rate load doles out | a doubt-loud flow into the overload.

In two small volumes of Poems, published anonymously, one in 1849, the other in 1852, many of the poems which compose the present volumes have already appeared.

What was Great Britain like when she won the battle of Waterloo?

"When a man writes a preface, he tries only to say an antithesis, and never thinks of the truth." (Charles James Fox).

Especially in the development of *Passages* I have workt with silences—with caesuras as definite parts of the articulation of the line, with turnings at the end of the verse, with intervals of silence in the measures between stanzas—related to phrasings and sequences of the whole.

My first memories are fragmentary and isolated and contemporaneous, as though one remembered some first moments of the Seven Days.

In English writing we seldom speak of tradition, though we occasionally apply its name in deploring its absence.

O Curator!

That fabulous polymath Samuel Johnson maintained that no man in his right mind ever read a book through from beginning to end.

The philosophical tradition is never entirely insensitive with respect to a great philosophical theory that often transforms it.

The most signal impact of feminism on the humanities and the social sciences has been a problematization of sexual difference.

This book is rather like one of those "Music Minus One" records of a concerto, in which the orchestral accompaniment is present but the solo instrument lacking.

Now that the succeeding century is well advanced into its second decade, it seems a good time to take a purchase and a perspective on the poetry of the twentieth century.

Mark Scroggins

The History of the Voyages of Scarmentado, set in the years 1615–20, is not one of Voltaire's best works.

Style is a terrible thing to happen to anybody.

I.

The Roué

If you were, then, like a snake
or some other animal to turn
on me. If you could
like an animal only speak
through mimes and gestures
and movements. If we all laid
down our cocktails and agreed,
this was where the line must
be drawn, no day without
a line drawn. I could display
myself along those lines,
but have no more desire
to be spectator to that display,
given the flaccidity, mushroom
pallor, general mopishness
and lack of spine, than
you. Your eyes are not
topaz, half-turning in the half-
light. Like a snake
rotating, cold scales
measured out across the room.
Is one always *helplessly* in love,
or is there such a thing
as calculated entrapment, half-
love in the half-light, love lite?
Writhe like a snake, turn
on me, flip me like
a switch. Off and on.

SUBURBAN URBANE

The bookstore invites, as the bar
      had beckoned. Beautiful airbrushed
      women sliding by on the roofs
of the cabs. An invocation or an
avocation, pulling you upright—straighten
      your back—and setting you
      in a place denominated yours.
The Klees and Hirsts, Koonses and
      Kandinskys, all demanded
      their requisite twenty-five seconds
apiece, the Puvises flattened themselves
into great swallowing walls of art
      and industry, philosophy
      and cider-pressing. You thought
you saw *La Belle Irlandaise* on the roof
      of a cab going by, candy-floss
      halo of burning hair. Somewhere
under the reservoir, divine vengeance
uneasily stirs, ripples out and sloshes
      into the basement's storage cages.

SARAH PALIN

oil trundles forward
shelving beneath breakers choking
naiads, sea-horses
the unpent rage
resentment without shape, distinction
      coal-dust clouds, knee-deep
coal dust
snapping at the air, the mouths
mimic a chorus of lip-
syncing backup singers, their
teeth desert-sun-bleached bones
lips cracked beneath
perfumed gloss
          the square
glasses and perfect hair
of necromancy
they rise from their seats,
those young men in evening
dress, fling their desire
at her feet *en masse*
           is she
a magician's robot? will it
rain tomorrow? what's making that noise
beneath the hood? did you find
the check-book? did he answer
the phone? what does this sign
mean? really?
        the sky

Mark Scroggins

did not fall, after all, nor
did the earth open
to swallow us up
lubricants are available
in gay profusion, scented,
flavored, even colored I'd
guess
      (I've stolen "gay profusion"
from Van Morrison, but suspect
he stole it first)

SPINNING CLASS

I lose my wind at the outset,
      regain it after
the second mile. Smike
      and chuff, pavement blab
and speed bumps scratch
      the undercarriage. What good
the criss-cross on the sky. Rings
      on the bar, the wiping rag
squeezed into a can. Sleep
      no more, the light is gone
and stiffens the flush
      of morning, angle of refraction
rate of dilation. The cubic
      centimeters was an urban
legend, but not the hundreds,
      thousands of Polaroids.
I want to swagger, read
      so hard, knotted ambition
a ball in my jeans pocket.
      The second mile is prelude
to the third. And so forth. An
      anaerobic ache, hairs plastered
against the nostril wings, ventral
      papillae tingled. *Spinning*
the best they can do, lights
      fluorescing on patched
and dyed, dewy scalps. Have you seen
      my wind.

The Heights and the Grange

It was only when the credits started to climb the screen
that we realized the show was really over, that the blond
boy would remain forever on the shore against
the sunset, his true love always out of reach. For my part
I wanted a simpler ending, one more conventionally "happy"—
a wedding even, though I know you snort
with a kind of superior contempt at those things.
It was time for dinner anyway, light dishes
for a warm July evening: asparagus and trout,
perhaps, and of course a salad. Watching a lover
move around the kitchen in the twilight,
before one turns on the lights, is comfortable,
like settling into a favorite chair with a book—
a novel maybe, just on the verge of trashy—
you've read a couple of times before. The protagonist
is darkly handsome; he has trouble keeping his hair
out of his eyes, doesn't know which of the women
throwing themselves his way actually loves him
for who he is, rather than for his unaccountable millions,
houses and steam-yachts and so forth.
He likes the red-haired one, but worries her pre-Raphaelite
mane is the sign of some kind of wildness—you know,
the sort of woman who'll break dishes in a rage,
maybe even slash the tires of his car. For her part
she doesn't know who her parents were, grew up
in an orphanage with stern but kindly nurses,
tried to keep out of the way of the priest
with the suspicious gleam in his little piggy eyes.

The twilight is all salmon behind the picture window
framing the trees, the lawn, the street and a couple
of street-lamps into—well—a picture. I considered the relation
of landscape painting, the *seeing* requisite to paint
a landscape, or rather, to *frame* it rightly, to the art
of landscaping, moving all those trucks and wheelbarrows
of earth, planting and mulching and nurturing shrubs
and trees, hedges and an occasional flower. All behind glass,
the vast incline of the lawn. We can't see Catherine, Linton,
or even the gormless Hareton; perhaps they're behind
the ha-ha, fumbling at each other's drawers in the gloaming.

Mark Scroggins

POST-TROPICAL

Consent to buckle, consent to rhyme.
Concretion stares the terminus
of unrepentent waverers, miniature
boskage tangled, vine and tenthrils.
Skyvine, grapevine, bacchic and grand,
the soil as sandy as the shingle.
      off the dial and aft
      the charts full moon
      lowering an angry lover
      heavenly judgment v.
      inept earthly remuneration
Raise or raze the roofbeam, stilt
those homes beyond my parents' reach.
Tongue-and-groove ceiling and walls,
tongue thrust—on the bed—into
emptiness, emptiness clutched. My restless
heart, careening imagination, straining after
vees of Canada geese. What rood to read.

Force-Feed, Force Field

Whatever comes up, gets drawn
in. See it here, shaped and trimmed
to manicure.

That two of three meanings come down
to *force*, energy, force to beat us
about the shoulders in the small
of the back, tack us like a crow
to the barn-door.

Force and erosion, resistance.
Moral.

That jaunty Herakles would cauterize
the harmless lizards' heads, throw
a lion's mandible over his own skanky
mane.

The mucous membranes tender against
the tubes, cold or chafing. Stripped
and straps. This air, look you, not good
for wild flowers.

A lawgiver from parts unknown, or parts
known. Club and nail, key
and rudder. Keys in massy bunches
bulging the jeans.

GOOD FRIDAY

Say it; it looks so easy.
The night is black, with
a chill. Half an hour ago,
two raccoons passed my chair,
a rust-red moth settled
on the desk, refused to mount
my finger. Tell it plain.
There is no silence
here. No silence.
Scratch, and breathe,
and hear the little animals'
high chitterings over the tires
on pavements. Over sand and
water. Over shards of stone
and chemicals and unfamiliar
bones.
      The palms, bushes
wrap around them, tense, push
up into the air. We cut
them back. Her sister's snoring,
breathy, faint, almost illegible,
keeps her awake she says. Machine-
hum of the cat, satisfied.

Easy. Plain. I hear animals
and mechanisms in the night.

No accounting for taste, Charles

said, nothing but the best,
the wholesale sharkskin
fork-tongue proliferation, leaded
and rounding, head down
to the tailwind, head-
wind driving past that
plateau where the ice-rocket
swerves, turns back, asks
the way and strikes a
tableau of passers-by laughing
and clapping like a dropped
tray back in lunch hour
taste, touch and see, the eyes
of the hand, rough
turbid propositions piled
on the counter like meat-
pies, yellow shrinks
the room despite the slate
of the trim and base-
board, the chemical gash
unnumbered invaders and
spreads across the pool.

OFFICE ROUTINES

We had prided ourselves on how promptly
we answered letters, but all that went
to hell when the new system was installed.
In the old days, correspondences maintained
between the planets and the viscera, politics
and the heavenly movements; now everything
keyed itself to one digital counter, blinking
and constantly picking up a stray minute
here or there. A three-legged dog trotted—
or whatever such a triped does—along
the highway, nosing the wind for a break
in the trafffic. We are told the new interface
is more "natural," "easier," more "intuitive,"
like picking up a stick and scrawling
the Tetragrammaton in the sand at the beach,
or falling off a log. Disorienting enough
to be working with a thermostat, adjusting
the speed of one's reflexes to some ideal
mean, shivering and sweating by turns, and
listening for the cries from the intercom
that will summon us doubleplusquick out
of our homey cubicles. Mine—since
you ask—is minimally but tastefully
decorated: a few family portraits, scent-
free potted plants, a bowl of candies unlikely
to go stale anytime soon, a poster of
Britney Spears at her most pleasingly
modest. The bell buzzes for us all, they

say, and calls us to the traps and objects
of somebody else's world. Voicemail
and instant messages, football scores,
stock reports, half-price clearances, fore-
closure sales and forced enclosures.

ARENA

The bouganvillea does not curl
in the acorn, the spores
of the ferns crowd our eyes.
She pressed small hands into
the wet sound, pulled
out shell-fragments, a kind
of wood (*white sand*) pulled back
her hair elaborate into a sort
of knot-work. Barometers of
jewelry and glittering leather,
infant ear-rings spider-web
hair knotted with sweat.
Arena is sand, to soak up
blood or oil or other
expensive viscous fluids.
My friends roar by, wave out
the windows (*cell phone*) traffic and commerce
printed our pages, the regular
menhir-delivery those days
interrupted only by postal holidays.
The retinas sutured—minute cables
of scar-tissue, nudges of concentrated
light—to the back walls
of her eyes (so blue!) (*freeze frame*) home movie
without editing, stretches of nothing
but static words like a camcorder
in a crowd (*radio on*) The "we" became
royal without our noticing, an axis

around which we spun to the brink
of nausea. Twelve steps, gingerly,
and fell flap upon the cheek-
bone. He was behind the wheel,
true, but he wasn't arrested:
a way to avoid being crippled,
at least, so he left the baby—dying—
behind; took up arms, bore arms,
brandished the gaudy stippled
drag of money's uniform.
Their whines of good faith figured
the orange plastic netting around
a construction site, where March means
spring impends, the heat settles down
on the flats. The Lord will know
his own; our sorting is superfluous.

SECURITIES & EXCHANGE

tracing the fireworks' roman
        candles' sparks falling listless
down humid air peonage drainage
        hand-work and black signage
coined the abstractions underneath
        whose mauve shadows he seized
homely comforts familiar pleasures
        weight on one foot he stood
along the deck a canted pivot
        and running slip to fall the rain
incessant dyeing from the west
        the branches a deeper ochre
to shift that load he needed
        something unlike the things the screen
flashed against his eyes bleaching
        his hands and broad forehead
nature alma mater alma genetrix pressing
        green out of the stems again and
again laughter at his hacking clipping cutting
        gestures against her venereal metastasis
the sweat-slick deltoids of the meter-reader
        bespoke pastimes more strenuous than
reading sitting writing over and over
        familiar laments for fallen securities
by this time year on year he spoke
        only to himself arguments sutured
then perforated by invisible projectiles
        of rhetoric cords fanned out

from some demented center ball-bearings
      swivelling like the hips of that
prosthetic girl who smeared her lipstick
      on his whitest collar sway backward
grass skirt approaching industrial zero

Mark Scroggins

Tennessee

The roadway cuts through billows
of impervious green, reveals
its slashes in walls of drilled
and dynamited rock.
Toward sunset, successive fields
of blue-gray pastel layer
the distance. Nodding
at the wheel. World under
glass. Bereft of friends, bereft
of short-term memory, she turns
the object over in her hands,
recounts again the self-same
half-dozen themes. Turds
and sodden toilet paper
boiled up from the sewer
cleanout, so that blue
flies hovered and buzzed
on the face of the lawn.
The upstairs never quite cools
down—books' bindings
stiffen, crack, flake. Verbs
in threes, like the Father Son
and Holy Spirit, Jesus Mary
and Joseph. When she turns
them over, they stiffen, flake.

Humanities Research

Flesh marble of the bath
laved their hair exfoliated their backs
so that two guttering candles
then one alone cast bright
ellipses on the conjugal ceiling.
The goal was to singing dance
across a shimmying quarter-deck
lightfoot passing from wall to rafter
while six discs shuffled them
from windy New Brunswick misty
Northumberland to melancholy swamps
of doo-wop the Romany klezmer
fiddle-accordian. Red pure as blood, though soluble,
        black and white checkerboarding
        the goofy pantomime faces of beasts
        and birds. A flushing of excrements as glib
           as the thrust of missiles or pounding
           expensive lubricated machinery.
Hat on head pen pressed in hand
he could bleach places names identifying
marks more surely off the page
than the collapsing building "vaporized"
eight hundred carcasses, shifting their
debits onto a separate account.
        Detailed expensive the automobile
        spins noise from the water
        beneath its tires its shining
        engine a sealed, solipsistic hum.

Exceeds its pellucid prose.
Skips its composition.
Stylometrics inferior says P. Arbiter
to close reading (*old news
deportment*).
Broken-backed similes to tie
floating pictures together
asserting unlikely consanguinity
she knits big words to little
a fishy taste to the water there
air conditioning pressing you into
a borrowed sweater on hundred-degree
days Measure that man's life out in linear
feet numbered boxes personal
effects stored in an off-campus
location: his reading glasses his silver-
handled stick his vast collection
of smoking pipes inscribed first
editions the elaborate custom writing-
desk and quaint typewriter displayed
behind a warning tape They must have
bumped
into one another going to and from
their interviews with surviving intimates
And it's all built on oil. Clowns and curling ivy
in marbled composition books, letters typed
and manuscript, carbon copies and browning

ancient xerography, right hand on the head
      of the youngest son. *His* son wanted to be an opera
          singer. The guy in the mailroom
              plays in a Tejano band. The *ah-hoo*
              of the polka, identical from Paris,
              Texas to Minneapolis.
          The sheeps' and goats' heads ($5.99 and
          $3.99) intended for some regional
          delicacy. Remove the fell. Layer the leg
            with slivers of garlic—all over. Somebody
else's coffee maker, someone else's
      dishes and towels. The torture garden
          is okay, but the computer pitted skips
          and drops out at the worst
              moments. The rain beats
          against the screens. The beautiful ringlets
of the Polish woman in the reading
room, with whom the whole cadre of pale-
bellied near-sighted note-
takers seemed to have fallen
in love. The caves are clammy dark
          and deep but the giant armadillo
          blue and pugnacious shaking
          spears from his back
          is a fake.

Mark Scroggins

HEINRICH SCHÜTZ

the sewer fires stench
across the road filtered
decay fug excrement tangle
the palms' warm musk

he buys a magazine
to break a large
bill funnels the change
to a woman whose

streaked hair and long-legged
nubile daughter dominated his
daughter's evening they sang
to bleating trumpets shuffling

sackbuts the voiceprint score
of dark huddled nativity
breached and dated copper
tang of tangled armpits

beaded foreheads scarified upper
arms the hard-drive packed
and shuffled beyond recognition
he knows the voice

before he sees her
face he bent abrupt
toggling hapless closed circuits
the bottom is what

you can't go down
from cantatas carols in
merciless ears blithely woven
glad tidings forced down

the Latin of dead
men's harmonies
       why is he so angry?
       what counts so deeply crazes
       their satisfaction in bouganvillea skyvine
       umbrella-tree live-oak ficus and mounds
       of leaves trembling themselves humus-ward?
       he keeps
up with the scene
or tries though names

years profiles slipstream reckless
past disposable icons and
income *how the old*
man keeps it up

Mark Scroggins

is beyond me voicings
toxic reductive tuneful at
once tracking unintended consequences
down their mapped or

tabulated detours
           what counts so keenly now?
           which evangelist spun it out
           best Passion According to Saint
           Whom? wondrous story of nails
           thorn wood tears wine betrayal
           verso broken
into paragraphs tabulated in
some vulgate some frank
tongue your justified margin

GEORGE BUSH

drink you, he says, drink my oil
consume my heat—break
     your ears on words
     of consternation, flails
of knotted cords, squeaky-clean
mandibles or hands—which if they took of
moderately, in antique measure, might
        break, unbalance or siphon off
the bile collected
        in those administrative bourses—
pearls we do not *feed* to swine,
        but display in
rapt aesthetic gestures,
        totems raised above the trees
flags whipped to shreds in a data
storm, Permian sirocco of leaves, pages
     register ribbons and plain paper
     facts—press your nose against the casement,
     little furry one, add your cry
to the bruit in the street, baked goods
     and costly *fruits de mer*
when nothing is unclean to us,
        each dish defiles
     by its meager gratuity,
        token leavings
and irrecoverable totals
        a bitter color, magenta
tonality—open my eyes, small friend,

and help me extract the obscurity
from my father's gates

Dental Records

Here before you, like Duncan's body
        in his bed or two bloody brothers
on a slab, is his signature
        on a piece of yellow paper, torn
obviously from a "legal" pad.
        Here are his reading glasses,
a cash register receipt he used
        as a bookmark, and wrote four
lines of a famous poem on.
        My eyes are gray; no they
aren't. Birds sing outside
        my window, but can't be heard
over the air conditioning. A flux
        of words or blood poured down
the back of our thighs, so that
        we clutched at any hem handy.
Her chin is square and steely,
        like the image engraved on a piece
of money. We choose them
        for features like that. Hydroponic
lettuce in a plastic tray, tasteless
        as bottled water. Why would it strike
you strangely if the philosopher, jetting
        in from some transalpine university, wore
a miniskirt and stilleto heels?
        When I knew him, she said, he was beautiful:
short and blond, his skin was white, his cheeks
        and lips were pink. Gray now, gray and hard.

29

I never notice money slipping away
       anymore; it never even shows up
on paper. Why don't you get those broken
       teeth fixed, she asked him: I want
to look like one of the people.

A Table of Green Fields

he died half-shaven, the first
     time in his life; asleep,
I track him,
     wandering thru woods, openings,
sudden bright meadows
     the night creaking of things
alive and made, flappings
     sounds beneath the threshold
of hearing, felt in the pelvis
     no one there, but that no
one speaks sounds: "why
     did you leave me, twisting on
that cranked-tight hospital
     bed? where have
I gone?" his watch sounds
     like a living thing
on my wrist, his face
     stares from my eyebrows,
wrinkled eyes—the cancer
     in the hip, the catheter,
the dizziness slide away like
     blurring memories—dim light
filtering the room, awake, legs
     taut from running, plucking
the counterpane.

Mark Scroggins

WHAT DO YOU MEAN, I ASKED THE POEM,

its gears for a moment at rest, steam
leaking from its boiler. Who
are you to ask, it replied, touching

my cheek with a human hand.
Where do you come from, I asked
the poem, marvelling at the shining
grooves behind it, which seemed

to vanish into the forest, but might
be snaking out across the plain
or climbing into the amber hills.
Who are you to ask, it murmured,

nodding its stiff mane, so like
the plume on Hektor's blinding helmet.
What are you for, I asked the poem,
but the poem had nodded off, drive-

shaft disengaged, bowels a muted
mechanical hum, carapace bright and impassive.
So I lay full-length on the grass beside,
moistened by the poem's breath, acrid, hot.

II.
PRESSURE DRESSING

An electric clap, and the sky shuts
down. And pours. My desires, like yours,
are I expect rather simple. Orality, say.
The windows are sheeted, the streets
glazed with water. I do not know
my desires by sight or name, suspect
licking and swallowing and tasting
are involved. We all want
to be loved—they say. Everything
is there for the eating, under the clouds.

Can you feel the muscle hardening?
Is it there? Is it tasty, or visually
satisfying, or moist? Where does it go
afterward? When someone shuts off
the lights. Clap clap. If this has
a history, it's news to me, but there
are more things I don't know than
things I do. They preened themselves,
evidently, on their *visual literacy.* Does
it move independently of the joint?

Mark Scroggins

Pretty ballerinas at the barre. At
the bar. I stretched, pirouetted,
and forced my feet into numbered
positions for about three weeks,
then pulled a muscle. Like facets
of a crystal. They twirl and dip
and swoon. Alone, the slim body
curves as with pain, or hunger,
or aspiration. *Reach for the stars.*
Where did I put my shoes?

A gravid female apteryx, in x-
ray: the four-pound body swollen
with a gross one-pound egg. What
system would account for thirteen
separate sorts of finch, thirteen
acts of special creation? Long dappled
grass, a highway paved with
linnets' wings. Discipline. You learn
to channel those nasty drives.
A word for it, Hegelian almost.

The Real Thing. *Das Es.* Look, but don't
touch. Don't see. One language alone,
he tells, won't do, but what's said
isn't worth the hearing. Some god
bends his graceful, rib-rounded
torso to touch some nymph. Instant
rerun. She has an idea for the muse,
sharper than she ought to be, more
determined by far than me. Father
Helios, all a-wobble.

Very like a whale. Or a wombat.
(Begin again.) The beautiful young
people once dazzled with their earnest
resolve. Today the coastal metropoles
crumble as sea levels centimeter ironic
upward. How much of that debt
is mine, how much yours? And who
do we pay it to? Era, earful, any time
of day. Others' letters delivered, speed
on to whatever shadowed box.

37

A touch on the audio screen and one
harsh word brings the whole evening
crashing down. I've been on edge,
you've been on edge, she's been
on edge—conjugation of inevitable
verb. The mystery of the lost meter,
to be rendered moot when the sea
percolates up through the limestone
and erases all our mistakes. Both
entrances blocked. Drive trains.

The natural posture is upright. Natural
position. Problem of the "natural." I toss
and turn, every night, to get you closer.
We run, whether in sunlight or rain,
to stand still. This damned—another—
book. Pieces, bite. *Shards.* How do
"ew" vowels evolve: my father pronounced
it "strown"? Toward the end, he
couldn't live in comfort, slept propped
up with a finger on the morphine trigger.

The dream of great icicles fallen, smashed
on the sidewalk. Not *on* her, impaling
or crushing, but she herself shattered.
The Church retreating, the license
plates "Christian." This night suspends
water, hums with stone. I see only
from machines. Signs at the foot
of Trümmelbachfälle, the fatal
dangers of drinking one's water
too cold. Ammonia through the ceiling.

The valley opens up below you as
you ascend. Rushes up toward the helmet-
camera'd lunatic youths, their parachutes
and mashed potatoes with ketchup.
To build a city up there, raveled together
with cables, perilous switchbacks, gravel
and chilled pure water. Obsessed
with food, one more of the seven
deadlies. I dreamed you sliding down
that hillside, turning twitching reaching.

Sound out Faerie horns, or pipes
that mark the general distribution.
Year of Jubilee, twelfth year
of memory, nearabouts the Day
of Atonement, in the neighborhood
of a sheer unlucky Friday. A cracked
piano or crazy hurdy-gurdy,
make some noise to crack
the torpor. Strings or wind, blow
the hair out of your bloody eyes.

What was that program? did you watch
it alone? stream it? tape it? scattered
mixtape faded on the dashboard,
wee heart ballpointed on the label
a mark of careless, hapless
love. That moment in the hospital
bathroom, your lips pressed together,
her body's angles beneath leather,
everyone outside traumatized by terminal
sentences, telescopes into the past.

Old man in the rain, flagging
a ride where no one walks; I move
in a haze of pride and stupidities,
not least my own. Half-staffed
flags, and the experts rushing
up from the lowlands of Florida,
miasmal, choking moral fen—
dream of heat, dream of fertile
crisp and juicy amnesia to offer
their blood-rusted ordnance at a price.

Sentry-man of liberty! Wise *senex,*
his bloated face a board of happiness
and good company. Our Lord, he
says, and The Words, he says. How
to watch them unfolding
their theater (tedious, paralytic)
on the multiply-refreshed glowing
screen. Tie the purest purchase
with meters of the reddest, seal
it with a manly kiss.

No chill in the air, no breath
of autumn. That tree bowed itself
and fell, already dead, understanding
the swarming bustle in its heart
had broken down, digested sinew
and skeleton. Flex, stiffen, snap. A pool
of still time, only the familiar hums
of the machinery. I can reach out,
turn my head in the air. Which is
transparent, which sounds alike.

Twitch out our hurts, our lusts,
little moments of bliss
and strife, stuffing and voiding
in turn, fast as we can lay
hands on the stuff. Have those distant
suns drawn an instant closer,
for all our multi-colored big-
budget imaginings? Eyes
to the stars, tip-toe in a trench-
latrine, slosh up to our ears.

The sky a dome, pierced and
traversed by zeppelins. Too many
stories. Too much prose, tracing
fluid and light. Turns, twists
movements from one end
of the room to the other.
I want to *zap,* shape-shift
away. The only opening
of green for miles, fenced
with buses, cars, broken metal.

No idea what I've been reading.
The page before me ripples
and shimmies like a scroll
under water, words connecting
with nothing before them, nothing
in my head. Relatable, they say.
He threw the dishes in the sink
to go out to the play, *Earnest*
or ernest, earnest of something
I can't quite grasp. Connect.

Knickers in a twist at the scent
of original sin. Twist in us all.
Taking upon oneself the default
gender, genre of sexuality,
Latinate endings that push us
back from the pantings and sweat,
funny twitches and odd-smelling
bodily fluids. Across his knuckles,
down his pants leg. Teeth catching
the lobe of my ear.

Confectioner's fantasy, dashed
with the sleek of depilatories,
the funk of the stripper's
pole. Rhetoric of the march, rhetoric
of three-quarter time. Can one speak
brokenness without evoking
Original Sin? do the angels only
bob, pirouette, and pass their candles
to welcome us to Candyland? *Gold-
Bären Himmel,* translucent rest?

Timeless isn't right—without time,
sans the density, ghosts and moving
shadows, invisible lines but palpable
of ruined and overbuilt buildings;
air empty of everything but
humidness, funk and fume
of currency and machines. Shall
I build me a history, brick myself
into a country house of leaves
and bindings? bind me, dark-hair.

At today's meeting we consider
the viability of "Achilles" as brand-
name—for what, yet to be decided,
but all rage aside. I nurse my own,
middle-aged petulance a poor
substitute for the righteous prophetic
stuff. Nobody shuffles paper anymore,
but someone always forgets to make
a tablet or phone. *Achilles* shoes?
Will they live long?

45

Mark Scroggins

We don't see the towns fly by
when we're on the pavement—a canal
away it's a different tax structure,
and they do things differently, maybe
don't speak the language. Can't say
I talk it much, anymore. Married
fifty years without a trace
of dissatisfaction, if you believe
the stories. I'd like to. Don't believe
much of anything these days.

Writing up against love, as the anaesthetic
wears off, pushing up against love
like the growth in her belly, against
its wall. Penstrokes not enough,
scalpel-strokes. Philosophy in the
bed, awakening to the dialectic
in the semi-private room. Enlightenment
as x-rays. No time for puns.
No time at all. Pen pushing against
time, against cancer, against love.

The trees, the bricks, leaves and fronds
wiped clean. A sudden shower.
Our minds and hearts were paused
last night in a circle of light, twinkling
reflection on the water, as the clocks
turned over and reset themselves.
Foolish new resolves. No, not
at all. No conversions are less
than turnings. Sometimes the walls
and passages fade to open.

The fish—three-inch, four- —dart back
and forth, muddy bottom a half-foot
beneath. They curve around
the Muscovy duck like courtiers
around a monarch. Sky
is clear, hot; it will be white
with clouds in minutes.
The dusk's yellow eye focuses
the weight of the day. The fish,
like all of us, seize what they can.

Do it again. Pleasure
in repetition, even as it
changes. How many times
have I heard that song, that turn
of phrase? The wholly new
is wholly alien. I don't like
the word *totality* any more
than you do, but it's the only
word that describes it right—
what I can't grasp, that is.

Oh shit I said as I began
to talk and heard myself, *it's
the voice from the whirlwind
again.* The teacher garbling
noises at Charlie Brown;
the morning announcements over
the intercom. Voice that makes
you lie down, sit up, roll
over. Can I ask you a question?
Do you hear at this frequency?

I am a cork-cutter, he said,
but an honest cork-cutter; I cut
my corks with skill and pride;
and then you made me look
above my station, and ruined
my world. Voice that seizes
your lapels. Not the sea, but
what floats over it. Those
dogs, those fucking dogs, and those
ramshackle mechanical wings.

Fierce dispute, not really, more like
a beatdown of all that's good,
and tender, and lovable, by chain-
fuelled inevitability. At least
I still have my eyes to read
by, if the sky's as dim
and grumbly as a basement
rafter. Back and forth
we writhe, insects beneath
some distracted hero's thumb.

Blocks of woods and stacks
of rebar; wee intricate repro-
ductions of famous paintings
and broken glass, packed
in a valise; the inevitable
smeared yawps of expression,
precise colored rectangles.
Some fifty pages of Victorian prose
painted over with the precision
of Persian miniatures.

The word of the day
is "embedded," which you may
remember as the word of about
a decade ago, then in common
use to describe military-
press relations, and often slurred
in bed with. But this muck
of a life?—I guess so,
I'm embedded all right, and in bed
with, and what have you.

What's that again? my hearing's
not what it used to be.
Neither is my eyesight, smell
or touch. Taste as questionable
as ever. Once it was as lithe
and flexible as an eel, that
tender prehensile organ of my
mind— Fooling myself again:
those songs are the best, change
that station right away.

Black and white furred lightning.
Or a matted cushion beneath
the table, drifts of hair
in everyone's drinks. We took
it all in stride, the catfights
and toilet accidents, like
the latest political scandal,
the bar mitzvah DJ with his head
between the thighs of a passed-
out fifteen-year-old.

Mark Scroggins

The sane woman in the attic
conservatory, the savage goth-
girl in white. Ravelling out
a stemma of those lightning
lines, a family tree
of utterances like tomahawks
splitting heads. Emotion alone
endures, like broken crockery
shuffled back into the cabinet,
moused among the fireplace ashes.

Reprieval—redemption—atonement—
all those big balloony words we used
to feel upon our pulses, they sound
like phrases in a faded legal brief.
The law used to present itself
as a structure that bore up
the whole of this fair fabric,
the visible world. Beat beneath
the chord changes, asphalt
beneath our tires.

The sky goes dark in the way
a computer-generated sky
does, the fires burn down, and
the lights dim. A breathless moment,
then the doors hiss open on a room
of palpable blue-black
darkness, the plaster casts
of the dead huddled, scattered,
petrified in moving, motionless
agony. The pet pig made her weep.

Voice like a trumpet, that never mutes
and never modulates: why whisper, why
pause, when you're seized up
in a paroxysm of passion, ready
to change the world? Tell me you
like it this way, tell me what
you like. Here's a book of diagrams
and positions, with directions
and everything. And bits of con-
versations, and distant pleasured cries.

The way one unit, bit of bowed
melody then splash of pizzicatto,
leads on to the next—the maze's
thread winding across the finger-
board, through the sound-holes
across the trembling air
to the piano, and back again.
To do that without moving
a muscle, no wince or
grimace. Slip from bar to bar.

Repeating one unit, bit of
melody, after another, redoubled
and stacked, shelved in a kind
of reverberant, humming silence.
You whisper against the pain, your
voice sends twinges down your
spine. Head filled and over-
filled against the morning's
chill, before the furnace hums
itself awake, dissipates.

Voice like woodwinds, or muffled
kazoos, nudging at the sides
of your head, packed with cotton
wool. Back aching, coiled all night
on a hard sofa. *We're not cops,*
we're not firemen. The face to
the monitor, backlit, is just
a haloed shadow, discoursing
shade. Speak, shadow—tell
me how to live, what to do.

Mired in the present tense, she saw
no way beyond the now, its vanishing
integuments and perpetual, sixteen-
frames-a-second replacements.
But we all moved in a *now,* back
then. Right now, it's that time
of year when the camphor-smell
of mothballs outmuscles
the Axe Body Spray, and all the muscles
disappear in a swath of bundling.

Right-ho, or some other mark
of agreement. Should I feel at home
among the men shuffling through
the toy soldier show, arguing
strategy and tactics, laying siege
to their childhoods? No game
for Rupert and poor fat
Newcastle, who closed up shop
and shipped out for Flanders, leaving
his Lambs dyed in their own colors.

The trees of life—evergreens, so they
say—are withered up through
the middle. Keen of a violin
harmonic, hesitant, hesitated, then
repeated. Drained of all desire
to move, to think, speak. Noise
of the late afternoon and the winding
echoes of commerce, spangling
across an air clear and bright
as an open major chord.

Bright splotches of white, as of bleach,
mildew, like coins thrown across
the leaning fence-timbers. A four-note
sequence—*fear-fear-fear-fear*—from some
bird punctuated, out of sync, by
intermittent basso *woofs*. The ordinariness
of it all—the bloody comfortable
daily: while my bones, wrapped in aching
and decaying flesh, silver at the verge,
the moment before it all falls apart.

Gravitas, Latin so happily adopted
in these our late flyaway days;
the words ought to weigh, bear down
and hold the page firm by their own
gravity. Ponderous; costive; the weight
in the bowels, the sense
of the world's ponderousness
pressing vertical down the whole
organism, which trembles, shivers,
sometimes—with a bit of luck—holds up.

57

Mark Scroggins

Hacking away, scraping and scratching
as if it were nothing more
than an unsatisfied itch, a shameful
personal grouse. Ruskin, we
are told, ranted out
the whole mystery of life
to set straight one godfearing
girl. Yes, It's personal.
And yes, the personal is always political,
whatever your oracle says.

No *yesses* or *nos*. Asked to answer,
the god's mouthpiece speaks
in koans, parables, or tricksy
cantos. Happier far the believer
with a firm, untranslated
text in hand. The Vulgate's
no longer legible to me,
all the Good News
has somehow soured
in my smoky mouth.

So when, as we trudge forward, does
neurotic misery finally become *ordinary
unhappiness?* And what did I
really mean when I said what I
thought I meant? The text
of scripture is plain enough,
if translated, but the interpretations
are without limits. No bounds
to your reading, no end
to your compulsion to repeat.

The grand façade, what a pompous
bit of nonsense! but we each
build our own little community—
walls, guard-house and so forth—
to get away from the desk in that
cubicle, get away from those
fluorescent lights. I want you
here—I want to be alone.
Spits of rain, occasional, endless
golden vomits of sun.

Mark Scroggins

Twenty years since he ended that run
on *Top of the Pops* with a whimper
and a bang both, and only now
we're seeing what was folded
in his wallet all the time. What bile
drove him blond, into that corner
out into mythology? Weights, ponders,
panders and whores—a blue guitar
(*I had that blue guitar*) on which
nothing at all was changed.

Heavy-set, then grown into thinness—
gaunt is what I want, hollow-eyed
and sharp-cheeked. Grin into
the mirror, reproduce yourself
for a hundred nodding friends.
Gone now, folded under, leaving
a spoor of snaps and phrases
to be fingered, riffled by voyeurs
interested or disinterested. And
a hole, of course, a hole.

It would break anyone, that bad
bad thing. Terrible awful thing, worse
than the worst you could imagine.
You're right, it's beyond me, beyond
my little stretch of mind, my wizened
and blinkered emotions. That pain,
that hole. Speaking back and
forth in tiny bursts, squeezed
little wads of pain. Break any-
one, bad bad awfulness.

Seat of emotions, seat of blood
and its mighty lunar circulation.
The scent still on my beard until
I washed and scrubbed, spouting
like some awkward marine mammal,
tore my short-sighted eyes
from the mirror to see you
standing behind, clutching at
your left breast. Mighty columnar
circulation, fountain of pain.

Life without drive, without a song,
a simple singing song, bit
of music to lift your spirits. Twitter
of bird-spirits around the leafage,
aria of water trickling and dividing
in air, coming together again.
Life, air, buoyant and rocking
on the balls of my feet, against
the weight of days the press
of years and sour months.

I had expected an apotheosis by
now, *Aufhebung* into the cloud,
level up, happy ending at the very least. It's
like a movie you've borrowed from the public
library, so nicked and smeared
the player keeps freezing, skipping
back to the beginning
of the segment. Breaks off
right at the funny bit, streaks
and scatters right at the throat-catcher.

True enough, no heroes around these
parts, spells or swords, rescues
or daring gambles. *Gemütlichkeit*
at best, adventures proxy. Tourist
to our own long drawn-out
vanishing, snap photos and post
sunny comments as we fade
into big data. He could be objective
about that. Smooth thigh across
his knees, doesn't enter into it.

Final performance this afternoon, end
of the run. Every song, every line suffused,
I'm sure, with anticipatory nostalgia—
never mind the hokum, absurd triple
rhythms, third-rate *histrio*'s
flesh-creeping ploys. Wish it were over
already. Wish it had never started.
all merely players, no more or less. Lover,
spouse, orphaned child, bereaved
mother. Cardboard masks, flesh masks.

Mark Scroggins

Not a drive, after all, no matter what
the game—its pinhead families, six-
passenger cars—might imply. *Journey*
a flawed if popular metaphor; time
to revive *struggle, battle, stage-
play?* The rolls were parceled out
far too long ago to change now.
I keep shuffling back and forth
before the podium—obsolete—
pantsless, with nothing to say.

Once, like some sexy myth, you meta-
morphosed from a tower of ivory
into a plunging, writhing rut-
weasel, right in my arms. Now
we turn into old people before our
very eyes. No time-lapse, speeded-
up film. Winding down, thickening
like some expensive gravy, bones
at the stock-pot's bottom. Something
to keep us warm, as we congeal.

That border is permeable, so we're
told, or semi-, or at the very least
shot through with portals. The magic
leaks out, like fumes from the sriracha
plant, brightens our day and makes our eyes
water. A blank wall, really, cinder-
blocks, and on the other side—there is
no other side. Everything, in the half-light
of the real, like a joke: the food is lousy,
the portions—harpied away—too small.

So many, stolid and resigned, crying,
begging, or lips trembling in assumed
stoicism, hoicked abruptly out of this life.
It was a low and dirty century,
even in its last third. The century
before was probably just as bad, but
I can't say, not having been there.
Poets sitting in cafés try to write
about love, and politics. Little
children dance and learn their lines.

Social animals, we huddle together
for the warmth, dew and drizzle
beading on our coats, thick and
scanty. The machinery keeps us alive
only so long. There was no cessation
of beeping, for instance, when she
died three years ago. They pulled
the tubes and hoses, dimmed
the lights, set out the cloth
and china as for a date, a mass.

Each item squirreled away, day
by day, year piled on year, aglommerates
itself into a mass, a mountain.
Daylight between the kitchen
utensils, the books, the thousand
greeting cards. I don't recognize
those names. Handfuls then armfuls
of papers shoved into heaps,
to be carted out of memory. My
life—their lives—in pages, pages.

The shape of the words in the mouth,
ground strange against the palate, letters
unfamiliar eldritch insects, St. Cyril's
coy and cunning invention. Pages upon
pages of them, piling into years
of staring and labor. My father
conned those pages once, now ash
and pulp. Shape of language, shaping
itself around ordnance, logistics, crime
and punishment, war and peace.

Walls, doors, a roof. To keep
the rain out. The dark out, keep
the dark at bay. A comforting shell
of lights, warmth, to arrange
the books, the knicknacks, the
accumulation. The overflow.
Turn from one to another
stolid brick to the hill,
concatenated angles against the
wind, skeleton of sticks on the beach.

Her baptism is complete, benediction
spun out in grave and common words,
rock-words that meet the ears
in the hushing echoes of Brahms,
piano-hammer and horsehair bow.
'Nother dying, another one
dead. In the shaded chapel's
aftermath, bubble of silence,
two policemen browbeat a homeless
lunatic with *Courtesy, Professionalism, Respect.*

Where am I? where am I going? Dark
and tunneled, as the light presses
weakly through the windows and the notes
flutter pizzicato from the other room—
"Summer" from the *Four Seasons,*
I think. This place is not my home.
At home no place. I think I want
to be alone in silence. No place
alone, no place quiet. Light presses
weakly; noise leaks through the blinds.

His skin, hands clawed to the chair's
curve, thewless, rooted, is clearer
than mine. Brush and clip, carefully,
arrange the lank hair. Within the brain-
pan, the humming sensorium hollowed
out and tunneled like a cheese.
If a lion could speak—an engine
seized up, rusted shut—and how
might you map, Herr Doctor Joyce, the
layered Hissarlik beneath that dome?

The poem is the cry of its
accumulation. The thing
itself and not about the thing—
or a chitter, scratch, fingernails
on the fretboard. *Trauma*
is wound, injury, sealed over
and callused until we barely feel
it aching, sullen and persistent.
Accumulation of paper, script,
possession; scar tissue.

The cry of accumulation, cry
of acculturation. Sifted layers
of things, *stuff,* gathered middens
gathering to themselves dust,
detritus. Wanting work, slain
by the enormity of the job
just comprehending. Documents
grant the equivalent, but
word-of-mouth hands-on
slurry of living.

Syntax of place, moving place
and shifting. Trammel me in another's
houses, under the lights of someone
else's pool. Push me down on
someone else's naugahyde
sofa; make me like it. Light
dismantled the gate, thrusts
a rented fourteen-footer
up the slides and around
the curves, treacherous, yours.

Clods of dirt against the polish of
pine, and flowers—whole, shredded
into petals—among the showers
of dirt. A mosquito on the officiant's
gleaming calf, mosquitoes thrusting
through the violinist's hose, raising
little hills of irritation. From some-
where, a brown spot on the white
of my shirt. No break in the sky's
gray, the endless prepositional phrase.

How to weave it all
together, with every year
that trundles by feeling more
and more alone, single under
this humid faceless broadening
sky—how to speak in unison,
chorally, it all together—single
voice, tenuous line across
the page of vast faceless
broadening grasses, humid.

Climactic, climacteric, humidity
lifting as the pain settles
in the bones and heart.
No running in the hallways,
ever, no change for the snack
machine: cat's droppings
in the puddle next the car
door. Nothing moves, no
running. Twigs and branches
arch the hallway, wet and alive.

Cobwebs in my eyes, across
my glasses, in the corners
of my mouth. Word-webs, thought-
webs, filaments of half-
remembered ideas, bits of
bitten-off phrases. To say
I love you is to quote
a thousand pop songs, hundred
thousand old poems. Mouth full
of threads, webs, speaking.

Somewhere you hear it, from snarled down
among those drafts and fragments, those pirated
and authorized editions (corrected, full
of misprints), those tangled stemmata—
the voice of a Moor strangling his girl-wife,
faint cries of an old prophet tied
to the gridiron, soft murmur
of a woman turned to wood
in water, then gold, then
dissolved in words again.

So you like it, do you? It appeals, it
fascinates? You don't know much
but you like what you know. Free-trade,
too, which gives the conscience
a break. The speed-bumps, breaking
the street's surface every fifty feet
or so, break your speed, break down
your suspension. Do you still
like it? I'm sure we have it all
in a larger size.

Easter Island, Williamsburg
Virginia. An almost empty
Day's Inn, dim large hall and
banquet room glittering for Christmas,
glittering for a wedding. Dusk,
the car nosing around *Presidents
Park* (*Washington, Adams, Jefferson*)
vast white busts heaving out
of the mist (*Harrison, Tyler,
Polk*). Crude, vast, white.

Warm and clammy night breath shut
out, the artificial chill calms and centers
us swathed in fabrics. A million tiny
sounds behind the glass, a dozen
murmurs. All falling imperceptibly
apart, frames missing between your
gestures, texts going astray. The night
settles down, calms like a big
warm parent. Shut out, behind glass,
shivering the layered varnish apart.

What do you want? What would make
you happier? Is it there? Do you want
me to turn this way, around? Is it
too dry? Prickly? Too rough? Is this
surface too slick, this corner too
shiny? Do you want to forget some-
thing, or remember, maybe? Is
it too soft this time around? Should
I turn it down? Again? Does this
make you uncomfortable? Too much?

Too many gone down. This time last
year, last week. A presence in the corner
of your mind, moving and laughing
maybe crying but anyway still
there, still stirring in the shadows—
and then nothing, stack of
fading snapshots, some of them
gummed together, wad of letters
laughed-over, wept-over, retinal
traces of a snuffed candle.

That node, that swelling, that unfamiliar
hardness. The sore, venereal,
that does not heal, stubbornly weeps
its way through salves and creams,
prescription and over-the-counter.
Set aside in the back of a drawer,
removed from everyday use.
Stones of the kidney and gall
bladder, blockages and constrictions.
That node, unfamiliar hardness.

Odd, using the same word—
beauty—for the sunset, for the canvas
some miserable wretch crouched
six months over, and for the way
her hair falls across the curve
of his forehead. Defect
of vocabulary, toolbox of words,
more like an adjustable wrench.
So many, *all* like that—*lovely,
sublime*—fit and don't fit.

The day is beaten out of us, the day
begins before we're ready. Cats
to be fed, checks written and sealed
and sent off with stamps. A machine
so vast we can't see, imagine
even the obscure and poorly-
lighted corner where we work
and live, by turns. The turning
numbers, marking day, night
when man's work.

Milling about in the hour before dawn,
or an hour after sundown. Pink limbs
splayed, damp, across a crumpled
blue sheet, a sheen of sweat,
sighing, across her belly. Who's
the chaperone here? who's driving
the bus, and what's to keep
them on the straight and narrow—
or at least in their own lane? Before
dawn, damp hair on that pillow.

The story is consolation. A hole
in your life is filled—momentarily—
by the fullness of the story, its happy
ending. To hear the story is
to escape, step out of your body
your chains and your prison-house.
Wander the green pastures, smell
the flowers and sheep-droppings
of the soul. Consolation for the smell
of sour urine, disinfectant: escape.

That roof was a sieve, a colander,
a tiled expanse of holes and crannies
for water seeking its level to pool
among the books and papers. Walking
that roof, dancing his bulk
to the tunes of hair-metal and
kiddy-pop. The water coming down,
washing away images and words
smearing all into pastness. Creak
of those boots I don't remember.

A massif, or blank flatness
visible barely through the trees, or
the sunbeams breaking angular
off the reservoir water, visible
glaring through the trees. Which quiver
as if shaking themselves in
the wind. Empty air, no moisture
and joined sounds, noises
of buses and autos, voices
from the blank pavements.

A rich mahogany, these pages
frittering off into stamps and
slivers of brittle trash. Libraries
across the land subside into
pulpish landfill. Words, transfigured
into scribbled marks, overprinted
lines. Spoken in front of desks,
chalked on walls, copied. The ink
lifts off the printout. It all
sinks into brown time.

Let it come down—in sepulchral
tones, with a plummy English
accent of course. Engraved in what
counts as a child's brain-grooves,
portals of the ears. Wind flexible
ductile branches concordant
leaf and sepal—seed industriously
and carefully distributed. Upas-
tree, anger outstretched mild
beneath that shade, beneficent.

That tortured, gored, and sprawling
horse—gray on white, news-
printed flanks. Or the violent
copulation of red and white
geometries clashing like blocks
or automobiles. Words to the
wise, poems for the illiterate.
Speaking to be heard, piling
canted cylinders on tilted
cyclinders, steel, glass, mud.

Simplest things last, or the basics
over and over again. To never get
the trick of it, the hang. Blossoms
in the streetlamps, brushing
my shoulder like a stranger
in a bar, mistaking me
for someone else. Motion
repeated, a touch. Strained
against the glassy margin,
smearing the same fingerprints.

Ha-ha to the old men, pretending
to be Lear, pretending to be
Falstaff. I know it's Poloniuses
all the way down. Something
to be said for trite but true.
Skronk of the bus-brakes, that mark
on the forehead *might* mean
something. What rude beast
rumbles under these streets, beneath
the antiseptic laundry rooms?

Mark Scroggins

Innertubes and rotting nylon tires,
rust creeps across the zinc'd
surfaces, crawls under fingernails.
Windows that flap open in a wind,
bang over the cold deserted
boardwalks. Manhattan to
Mayberry, prosthetic neighbor-
liness. Angry bellows from a car-
window, the horns' uncanny affect,
like parrots repeating Keats.

The breath, the in and
out, the threading repetition,
carefully shaping melody over
the barely contained excitement
of drums and bass—ambition,
vision, cathedral rising
from murky slopping depths,
arches and pillared carvings
of noise, perception, melody, pulsed
heat and stammered song.

Smile, cant your head, cant
the phone so everything's fashionably
canted. Tear the fringes off
your face, expose those sprawls
of pale and flaccid skin—
ruptures of age, crevices and
depressions never in the light
before. Watch the years
wobble, indecent pudencies
of skin and fat and stubble.

That old ivory tower, more than
a century now, where the silverback
squats—sunk in impotence and
belatedness. The happy ironist swoons
along the street, smiling and
greeting, shaking hands enjoying
the views. Which, after all, are
always changing. New multicolored
vistas and gleaming screen-
shots as you browse and refresh.

Tangle, a snarl in the auburn
threads, improper division in the
wires. Flattening iron, make straight
the way and level the little
hills. Curled arpeggios, twists
and pining curls. Fiddleheads.
An arc, graceful, between one sector
of horizon and an immeasurable
other. Tug and weep, whimper—
snarl to silence, curve.

It eats us all, those gears and
wheels, concatenated struts,
organs, levers, flesh, pulleys.
Measure the days, hours, the pounds
and ounces—counted off against some
great clockwork machine behind
it all, measuring it all. She turns
in the dark, the last moments
before dawn begins to soften
the black. Warmth pulsing, ticking.

Acknowledgments

Some of these poems have been previously published in the following periodicals:

The Cultural Society: "Præfatio ad Lectorem," "The Roué," "The Heights and the Grange," "Force Feed, Force Field," "Office Routines," "Arena," "Tennessee," "George Bush," "'What do you mean, I asked the Poem,'" and stanzas from *Pressure Dressing*

Cloud Rodeo: "Post-tropical"

Marsh Hawk Review: "Arena" and "Humanities Research"

Golden Handcuffs Review: "Heinrich Schütz"

FlashPoint: stanzas from *Pressure Dressing*

Good Foot: "A Table of Green Fields"

I am deeply grateful to all their editors.

"The Roué," "The Heights and the Grange," "Post-tropical," "Force Feed, Force Field," "Good Friday," and "'What do you mean, I asked the poem'" appeared in the anthology *Litscapes: Collected US Writings 2015,* edited by Caitlyn M. Alvarez and Kass Fleisher (Normal, IL: Steerage Press, 2015). Stanzas from *Pressure Dressing* appeared in *Great Writers Occupy Golden Handcuffs Review: Anthology of the New,* edited by Lou Rowan (Seattle: Golden Handcuffs Review Publications, 2015).

About the Author

MARK SCROGGINS was born in an American military hospital in Frankfurt, West Germany, as—quite coincidentally—Theodor Adorno prepared to deliver lectures on "History and Freedom" across town at the Johann Wolfgang Goethe-Universität. He spent his childhood on various army bases before settling in Clarksville, Tennessee. He taught for many years at Florida Atlantic University in Boca Raton, and now lives in Montclair, New Jersey, and Manhattan.

Scroggins has published critical monographs on the poet Louis Zukofsky and the fantasist Michael Moorcock, as well as a biography of Zukofsky. His essays and reviews have been collected in *Intricate Thicket: Reading Late Modernist Poetries* (University of Alabama Press, 2015) and *The Mathematical Sublime: Writing About Poetry* (MadHat Press, 2016). He has most recently edited a selection of the erotic poetry of Algernon Charles Swinburne, *Our Lady of Pain: Poems of Eros and Perversion.*

As an undergraduate at Virginia Tech, Scroggins wrote iambic pentameters for the "New Formalist" Wyatt Prunty; A. R. Ammons directed his MFA thesis at Cornell University. His first collection of poems, *Anarchy* (Spuyten Duyvil, 2003), was followed by *Torture Garden: Naked City Pastorelles* (The Cultural Society, 2011) and *Red Arcadia* (Shearsman, 2012). He is presently at work on a long serial poem entitled (perhaps provisionally) *Zion Offramp.*

www.ingramcontent.com/pod-product-compliance
Lightning Source LLC
Chambersburg PA
CBHW021408090426
42742CB00009B/1054